$\mathcal{I}$n 1883 Clau[de Monet moved to] a small villa[ge called Giverny. He] rented the house [and lived there] for the final forty [years of his life. He bought] the property in 18[ ] [purchas]ed the parcel that he would convert into a waterlily pond. An avid gardener, Monet spent countless hours and funds cultivating his massive flower garden and precious pond. In fact, while Monet completed hundreds of canvases during his many years at Giverny, he claimed that his carefully tended flower and waterlily gardens were his greatest masterpieces. Today, the gardens are well maintained according to Monet's original designs.

Photographer and gardener Elizabeth Murray lived at Giverny in 1985 and worked in the famous gardens in exchange for room and board. She returns regularly to photograph them, bringing to her subject an intimate knowledge of Monet's color schemes, patterns, and use of light, which he employed in creating his gardens as well as his paintings. Her photographs are magical, romantic, and timeless—one expects to see Monet himself, poised with palette and brush, standing among the profusion of blooms so beautifully framed by Murray's camera.

Elizabeth Murray is the author of *Monet's Passion: Ideas, Inspiration, and Insights from the Painter's Gardens* (Pomegranate Artbooks, 1989).

Photographs by Elizabeth Murray

~ 1998 ~

MONET'S GARDENS

Pocket Calendar

POMEGRANATE CALENDARS & BOOKS

Monet's Gardens
Catalog No. 98202

Published by Pomegranate Calendars & Books
Box 6099, Rohnert Park, California 94927

Front cover: Fragrant pink roses are trained to cascade over umbrella-like structures, adding height and romance to Monet's garden. Underplanted blooms offer a stunning counterpoint in red and violet hues.

Cover design by Elizabeth Key
Printed in Korea

January at a Glance

S	M	T	W	T	F	S
				1	2	3
4	5	6	7	8	9	10
11	12	13	14	15	16	17
18	19	20	21	22	23	24
25	26	27	28	29	30	31

After painting, Monet's chief recreation is gardening. In his domain at Giverny, and in his Japanese water garden across the road . . . , each season of the year brings its appointed and distinguishing color scheme. Nowhere else can be found such a prodigal display of rare and marvelously beautiful color effects, arranged from flowering plants gathered together without regard to expense from every quarter of the globe.

—Wynford Dewhurst, *Impressionist Painting: Its Genesis and Development*, 1904

Monet's famed waterlily pond, mirroring the sky and surrounding foliage, treats the eye to a natural impressionistic masterpiece. In the background, lavender and white wisteria crown the graceful Japanese footbridge.

New Moon

29 *mon*

30 *tue*

31 *wed*

New Year's Day

1 *thu*

2 *fri*

3 *sat*

4 *sun*

January

mon **5**   *First Quarter*

---

tue **6**

---

wed **7**

---

thu **8**

---

fri **9**

---

sat **10**

---

sun **11**

Full Moon

12 *mon*

13 *tue*

14 *wed*

Martin Luther King Jr.'s Birthday

15 *thu*

16 *fri*

17 *sat*

18 *sun*

January

mon **19**   Martin Luther King Jr.'s Birthday (Observed)

---

tue **20**   Last Quarter

---

wed **21**

---

thu **22**

---

fri **23**

---

sat **24**

---

sun **25**

---

26 *mon*

27 *tue*

New Moon   **28** *wed*

29 *thu*

30 *fri*

31 *sat*

1 *sun*

S	M	T	W	T	F	S
1	2	3	4	5	6	7
8	9	10	11	12	13	14
15	16	17	18	19	20	21
22	23	24	25	26	27	28

The richness I achieve comes from nature, the source of my inspiration. Perhaps my originality boils down to being a hypersensitive receptor, and to the expediency of a shorthand by means of which I project on a canvas, as if on a screen, impressions registered on my retina.

—Claude Monet

Along the narrow gravel path leading to Monet's second studio, a brilliant border of white, pink, and red asters and cosmos contrasts beautifully with a bed of golden-toned sunflowers, marigolds, and dahlias.

2 *mon*

First Quarter 3 *tue*

4 *wed*

5 *thu*

6 *fri*

7 *sat*

8 *sun*

February

mon **9**

tue **10**

wed **11**   *Full Moon*

thu **12**   *Lincoln's Birthday*

fri **13**

sat **14**   *Valentine's Day*

sun **15**

Presidents' Day

16 *mon*

---

17 *tue*

---

18 *wed*

Last Quarter

19 *thu*

---

20 *fri*

---

21 *sat*

Washington's Birthday

22 *sun*

February/March

mon **23**

tue **24**

wed **25**   Ash Wednesday

thu **26**   New Moon

fri **27**

sat **28**

sun **1**

S	M	T	W	T	F	S
1	2	3	4	5	6	7
8	9	10	11	12	13	14
15	16	17	18	19	20	21
22	23	24	25	26	27	28
29	30	31				

[The pond is spanned by] an arched wooden bridge painted green, near which Monet sets up his easel. . . . The whole thing comes together to create a setting that enchants us rather than inspiring our awe, a dreamlike setting that is extremely oriental.

—Louis Vauxcelles, "An Afternoon Visit with Claude Monet," *L'Art et les Artistes*, December 1905

Above the waterlily pond, a lacy canopy of intermingled white and lavender wisteria gracefully veils the trellis over the arched Japanese footbridge.

March

mon **2**

---

tue **3**

---

wed **4**

---

thu **5**   *First Quarter*

---

fri **6**

---

sat **7**

---

sun **8**

---

9 *mon*

10 *tue*

11 *wed*

12 *thu*

Full Moon   **13** *fri*

14 *sat*

15 *sun*

March

mon 16

tue 17   St. Patrick's Day

wed 18

thu 19

fri 20   Vernal Equinox 7:55 P.M. (GMT)

sat 21   Last Quarter

sun 22

23 *mon*

---

24 *tue*

---

25 *wed*

---

26 *thu*

---

27 *fri*

New Moon   **28** *sat*

---

29 *sun*

March/April

mon **30**

tue **31**

wed **1**

thu **2**

fri **3**   *First Quarter*

sat **4**

sun **5**   *Palm Sunday*

S	M	T	W	T	F	S
			1	2	3	4
5	6	7	8	9	10	11
12	13	14	15	16	17	18
19	20	21	22	23	24	25
26	27	28	29	30		

Imagine every color of a palette, all the tones of a fanfare. This is Monet's garden. . . . Everywhere you turn, at your feet, over your head, at chest height, are pools, festoons, hedges of flowers, their harmonies at once spontaneous and designed and renewed at every season.

        —Arsène Alexandre, "Monet's Garden,"
              Le Figaro, August 9, 1901

Old-fashioned pink peonies and foxglove mingle harmoniously with bearded iris in the shade of an apple tree.

A p r i l

mon **6**

---

tue **7**

---

wed **8**

---

thu **9**

---

fri **10**

Good Friday
Passover (begins at sundown)

---

sat **11**

Full Moon

---

sun **12**

Easter Sunday

Easter Monday (Canada)   **13** *mon*

14 *tue*

15 *wed*

16 *thu*

17 *fri*

18 *sat*

Last Quarter   **19** *sun*

April

mon **20**

---

tue **21**

---

wed **22**   *Earth Day*

---

thu **23**

---

fri **24**

---

sat **25**

---

sun **26**   *New Moon*

---

27 *mon*

28 *tue*

29 *wed*

30 *thu*

1 *fri*

2 *sat*

First Quarter   **3** *sun*

M a y

mon **4**

---

tue **5**   *Cinco de Mayo*

---

wed **6**

---

thu **7**

---

fri **8**

---

sat **9**

---

sun **10**   *Mother's Day*

May at a Glance

S	M	T	W	T	F	S
					1	2
3	4	5	6	7	8	9
10	11	12	13	14	15	16
17	18	19	20	21	22	23
24	25	26	27	28	29	30
31						

It took me some time to understand my water-lilies. . . . I had planted them for the pleasure of it; I was growing them without thinking of painting them. A landscape doesn't get under your skin in one day. And then all of a sudden I had the revelation of how enchanting my pond was. I took up my palette. Since then I've hardly had any other subject.

—Claude Monet

Jewellike pink-and-white waterlilies sparkle on the surface of the reflecting pond. Monet insisted that the pond be kept clear as a mirror and that the spreading waterlily pads be trimmed in circular patterns.

M a y

mon **11**   *Full Moon*

---

tue **12**

---

wed **13**

---

thu **14**

---

fri **15**

---

sat **16**   *Armed Forces Day*

---

sun **17**

Victoria Day (Canada)   **18** *mon*

Last Quarter   **19** *tue*

---

20 *wed*

---

21 *thu*

---

22 *fri*

---

23 *sat*

---

24 *sun*

M a y

mon **25**

Memorial Day (Observed)
New Moon

tue **26**

wed **27**

thu **28**

fri **29**

sat **30**

sun **31**

J u n e

1 *mon*

First Quarter   **2** *tue*

3 *wed*

4 *thu*

5 *fri*

6 *sat*

7 *sun*

June

mon **8**

---

tue **9**

---

wed **10**   *Full Moon*

---

thu **11**

---

fri **12**

---

sat **13**

---

sun **14**   *Flag Day*

S	M	T	W	T	F	S
	1	2	3	4	5	6
7	8	9	10	11	12	13
14	15	16	17	18	19	20
21	22	23	24	25	26	27
28	29	30				

After painting, Monet's chief recreation is gardening. In his domain at Giverny, and in his Japanese water garden across the road . . . , each season of the year brings its appointed and distinguishing color scheme. Nowhere else can be found such a prodigal display of rare and marvelously beautiful color effects, arranged from flowering plants gathered together without regard to expense from every quarter of the globe.

—Wynford Dewhurst, *Impressionist Painting: Its Genesis and Development*, 1904

A delightful jumble of bearded iris in predominantly rosy purple, lavender blue, and starry white is neatly edged by soft mounds of lilac aubrieta. Flames of crimson Oriental poppies boldly punctuate these cool colors.

June

mon **15**

tue **16**

wed **17**   Last Quarter

thu **18**

fri **19**

sat **20**

sun **21**   *Father's Day*
                                    Summer Solstice 2:03 P.M. (GMT)

22 *mon*

23 *tue*

New Moon   **24** *wed*

25 *thu*

26 *fri*

27 *sat*

28 *sun*

mon **29**

---

tue **30**

---

wed **1**   *Canada Day (Canada)*
                                            First Quarter

---

thu **2**

---

fri **3**

---

sat **4**   *Independence Day*

---

sun **5**

July at a Glance

S	M	T	W	T	F	S
			1	2	3	4
5	6	7	8	9	10	11
12	13	14	15	16	17	18
19	20	21	22	23	24	25
26	27	28	29	30	31	

*For months at a time, this artist [Monet] forgets
that Paris even exists; his gladioli and dahlias
sustain him with their superb refinements—but
cause him to forget civilization.*

> —Arsène Alexandre, "Monet's Garden,"
> *Le Figaro,* August 1901

Hot pink cosmos *(Cosmos bipinnatus)* and white-tipped dahlias seem to
float above an airy, delicate stand of white rose asters.

July

mon **6**

---

tue **7**

---

wed **8**

---

thu **9**   *Full Moon*

---

fri **10**

---

sat **11**

---

sun **12**

July

13 *mon*

14 *tue*

15 *wed*

Last Quarter   **16** *thu*

17 *fri*

18 *sat*

19 *sun*

July

mon **20**

---

tue **21**

---

wed **22**

---

thu **23**   *New Moon*

---

fri **24**

---

sat **25**

---

sun **26**

---

27 *mon*

28 *tue*

29 *wed*

30 *thu*

First Quarter   **31** *fri*

1 *sat*

2 *sun*

S	M	T	W	T	F	S
						1
2	3	4	5	6	7	8
9	10	11	12	13	14	15
16	17	18	19	20	21	22
23	24	25	26	27	28	29
30	31					

*The garden is not the luxury hobby of some
property owner, created to show off the quality
of his seeds; it is the retreat of an artist, and the
flowers are his companions. He wants to be able
to caress them as he goes by, to feel them close to
him, surrounding him, friendly and beneficent
parts of his life.*

—Maurice Kahn, "Claude Monet's Garden,"
Le Temps, June 7, 1904

Monet's pink stucco house is accented with green shutters and a rose-covered trellis that runs the length of the porch. The blue-and-white-curtained French door leads to Monet's kitchen, from which trays of food were often carried to the garden for family picnics.

3 *mon*

4 *tue*

5 *wed*

6 *thu*

7 *fri*

Full Moon   **8** *sat*

9 *sun*

August

mon **10**

tue **11**

wed **12**

thu **13**

fri **14**   Last Quarter

sat **15**

sun **16**

17 *mon*

18 *tue*

19 *wed*

20 *thu*

21 *fri*

New Moon   **22** *sat*

23 *sun*

August

mon **24**

---

tue **25**

---

wed **26**

---

thu **27**

---

fri **28**

---

sat **29**

---

sun **30**   *First Quarte*

---

31 *mon*

1 *tue*

2 *wed*

3 *thu*

4 *fri*

5 *sat*

Full Moon

6 *sun*

September

mon **7**   *Labor Day (U.S. and Canada)*

---

tue **8**

---

wed **9**

---

thu **10**

---

fri **11**

---

sat **12**

---

sun **13**   *Last Quarte*

S	M	T	W	T	F	S
		1	2	3	4	5
6	7	8	9	10	11	12
13	14	15	16	17	18	19
20	21	22	23	24	25	26
27	28	29	30			

I have no other wish than to mingle more closely with nature, and I aspire to no other destiny than to work and live in harmony with her laws. . . . Nature is greatness, power, and immortality; compared with her, a creature is nothing more than a miserable atom.

—Claude Monet

On the edge of the waterlily pond, lilac puffs of meadow rue *(Thalictrum aquilegifolium)* dance with graceful spikes of blue-and-white lupine above the distinctive heart-shaped leaves of sweet coltsfoot *(Petasites japonicus)*.

September

mon **14**

tue **15**

wed **16**

thu **17**

fri **18**

sat **19**

sun **20**   *Rosh Hashanah (begins at sundown)*
                      New Moon

21 *mon*

---

22 *tue*

Autumnal Equinox 5:37 A.M. (GMT) **23** *wed*

---

24 *thu*

---

25 *fri*

---

26 *sat*

---

27 *sun*

---

mon **28**   *First Quarter*

tue **29**   *Yom Kippur (begins at sundown)*

wed **30**

thu **1**

fri **2**

sat **3**

sun **4**

S	M	T	W	T	F	S
				1	2	3
4	5	6	7	8	9	10
11	12	13	14	15	16	17
18	19	20	21	22	23	24
25	26	27	28	29	30	31

I have painted so many of these waterlilies, always shifting my vantage point, changing the motif according to the seasons of the year and then according to the different effects of light the seasons create as they change. And, of course, the effect does change, constantly, not only from one season to another, but from one minute to the next as well, for the water flowers are far from being the whole spectacle; indeed, they are only its accompaniment. The basic element of the motif is the mirror of water, whose appearance changes at every instant. . . .

—Claude Monet

Monet's water garden tapestry is woven with many textures, shapes, and hues. Here, yellow, white, and acid green tones mingle with the dappled reflections of blue sky glimpsed through a lacy curtain of deep green foliage.

October

mon 5   *Full Moon*

---

tue 6

---

wed 7

---

thu 8

---

fri 9

---

sat 10

---

sun 11

Columbus Day
Thanksgiving Day (Canada)
Last Quarter

12 *mon*

13 *tue*

14 *wed*

15 *thu*

16 *fri*

17 *sat*

18 *sun*

October

mon **19**

---

tue **20**   New Moon

---

wed **21**

---

thu **22**

---

fri **23**

---

sat **24**   United Nations Day

---

sun **25**

October/November

26 *mon*

27 *tue*

First Quarter   **28** *wed*

29 *thu*

30 *fri*

Halloween   **31** *sat*

1 *sun*

S	M	T	W	T	F	S
1	2	3	4	5	6	7
8	9	10	11	12	13	14
15	16	17	18	19	20	21
22	23	24	25	26	27	28
29	30					

*. . . This decorative vision is a relief after one has
wandered through the garden, laid out as it is like
a palette, where the flower beds are arranged in
magically brilliant colors, and where one's glance
is dazzled by polychromatic vibrations. This
whole establishment at Giverny represents an
ambiance which the painter has arranged for
himself; and for him, to live there is a constant
advantage for his work. . . . His workshop—is
nature itself.*

—Maurice Guillemot, "Claude Monet,"
La Revue illustrée, March 15, 1898

In front of Monet's house at Giverny, red and pink tulips burst through a
sea of vivid blue forget-me-nots. In the foreground, spears of purple bearded
iris, mounds of golden English wallflowers, and a border of lilac aubrieta
provide a regal color combination.

2 *mon*

Election Day   **3** *tue*

Full Moon   **4** *wed*

---

5 *thu*

---

6 *fri*

---

7 *sat*

---

8 *sun*

November

mon **9**

tue **10**

wed **11**
                                   Veterans Day
Remembrance Day (Canada)
Last Quarter

thu **12**

fri **13**

sat **14**

sun **15**

16 *mon*

17 *tue*

18 *wed*

New Moon   **19** *thu*

20 *fri*

21 *sat*

22 *sun*

November

mon **23**

tue **24**

wed **25**

thu **26**   *Thanksgiving Day*

fri **27**   *First Quarter*

sat **28**

sun **29**

30 *mon*

1 *tue*

2 *wed*

Full Moon   **3** *thu*

4 *fri*

5 *sat*

6 *sun*

December

mon **7**

---

tue **8**

---

wed **9**

---

thu **10**   *Last Quarter*

---

fri **11**

---

sat **12**

---

sun **13**   *Hanukkah (begins at sundown)*

S	M	T	W	T	F	S
		1	2	3	4	5
6	7	8	9	10	11	12
13	14	15	16	17	18	19
20	21	22	23	24	25	26
27	28	29	30	31		

This is where Claude Monet lives, in this never-ending feast for the eyes. It is just the environment one would have imagined for this extraordinary painter of the living splendor of color, . . . this man who has touched the intangible, expressed the inexpressible, and whose spell over our dreams is the dream that nature so mysteriously enfolds.

—Octave Mirbeau, "Claude Monet," *L'Art dans les deux mondes*, March 7, 1891

Fragrant pink roses are trained to cascade over umbrella-like structures, adding height and romance to Monet's garden. Underplanted blooms offer a stunning counterpoint in red and violet hues.

mon **14**

tue **15**

wed **16**

thu **17**

fri **18**   *New Moon*

sat **19**

sun **20**

21 *mon*

Winter Solstice 1:56 A.M. (GMT) **22** *tue*

---

23 *wed*

---

24 *thu*

Christmas Day **25** *fri*

Boxing Day (Canada)
First Quarter **26** *sat*

---

27 *sun*

December/January

mon **28**

tue **29**

wed **30**

thu **31**

fri **1**   *New Year's Day, 1999*

sat **2**   *Full Moon*

sun **3**

1 9 9 9   a t   a   G l a n c e

January
S	M	T	W	T	F	S
					1	2
3	4	5	6	7	8	9
10	11	12	13	14	15	16
17	18	19	20	21	22	23
24	25	26	27	28	29	30
31						

February
S	M	T	W	T	F	S
	1	2	3	4	5	6
7	8	9	10	11	12	13
14	15	16	17	18	19	20
21	22	23	24	25	26	27
28						

March
S	M	T	W	T	F	S
	1	2	3	4	5	6
7	8	9	10	11	12	13
14	15	16	17	18	19	20
21	22	23	24	25	26	27
28	29	30	31			

April
S	M	T	W	T	F	S
				1	2	3
4	5	6	7	8	9	10
11	12	13	14	15	16	17
18	19	20	21	22	23	24
25	26	27	28	29	30	

May
S	M	T	W	T	F	S
						1
2	3	4	5	6	7	8
9	10	11	12	13	14	15
16	17	18	19	20	21	22
23	24	25	26	27	28	29
30	31					

June
S	M	T	W	T	F	S
		1	2	3	4	5
6	7	8	9	10	11	12
13	14	15	16	17	18	19
20	21	22	23	24	25	26
27	28	29	30			

July
S	M	T	W	T	F	S
				1	2	3
4	5	6	7	8	9	10
11	12	13	14	15	16	17
18	19	20	21	22	23	24
25	26	27	28	29	30	31

August
S	M	T	W	T	F	S
1	2	3	4	5	6	7
8	9	10	11	12	13	14
15	16	17	18	19	20	21
22	23	24	25	26	27	28
29	30	31				

September
S	M	T	W	T	F	S
			1	2	3	4
5	6	7	8	9	10	11
12	13	14	15	16	17	18
19	20	21	22	23	24	25
26	27	28	29	30		

October
S	M	T	W	T	F	S
					1	2
3	4	5	6	7	8	9
10	11	12	13	14	15	16
17	18	19	20	21	22	23
24	25	26	27	28	29	30
31						

November
S	M	T	W	T	F	S
	1	2	3	4	5	6
7	8	9	10	11	12	13
14	15	16	17	18	19	20
21	22	23	24	25	26	27
28	29	30				

December
S	M	T	W	T	F	S
			1	2	3	4
5	6	7	8	9	10	11
12	13	14	15	16	17	18
19	20	21	22	23	24	25
26	27	28	29	30	31	

Personal Information

Name _____

Address _____

City _____ *State* _____ *Zip* _____

Phone _____

Fax _____

E-mail _____

In case of emergency, please notify:

Name _____

Address _____

City _____ *State* _____ *Zip* _____

Phone _____

Medical Information:

Physician's name _____

Physician's phone _____

Health insurance company _____

Plan number _____

Allergies _____

Other _____

Other Information:

Driver's license number _____

Car insurance company _____

Policy number _____